Elizabeth Jennings

CELEBRATIONS
and
ELEGIES

CARCANET NEW PRESS
Manchester

For Aileen and Desmond

First published in 1982 by
CARCANET NEW PRESS LIMITED
330 Corn Exchange
Manchester M4 3BG

*The author gratefully acknowledges financial assistance from
the Southern Arts Association.*

British Library Cataloguing in Publication Data

Jennings, Elizabeth
 Celebrations and elegies
 I. Title
 821'. 914   PR6060.E/

ISBN 0-85635-360-4

*The publisher acknowledges the financial assistance of
the Arts Council of Great Britain.*

Printed in Great Britain by Short Run Press Ltd, Exeter

CELEBRATIONS & ELEGIES

CONTENTS

GOINGS

A packet of hurried letters, nervous gestures
To do with fingers, voices high and low
But out of key, eyes afraid to meet eyes—
　　　All this meaning "Go".

A child might hug or rush into its silence.
This is the fear of life not fear of death,
And the promises that distances mean nothing
　　　Already out of breath.

O our walls are painted with partings we don't notice,
Our minds are galleries of looks averted.
Perhaps the cord was never cut completely
　　　And those birth pangs were started

In a universe that's vast with a unique
Structure of inter-connections—star and steeple,
Storm and brain cell. We are born to break.
　　　We are departing people.

AUTUMN

Fragile, notice that
As autumn starts, a light
Frost crisps up at night
And next day, for a while,
White covers path and lawn.
"Autumn is here, it is,"
Sings the stoical blackbird
But by noon pure gold is tossed
On everything. Leaves fall
As if they meant to rise.
Nothing of nature's lost,
The birth, the blight of things,
The bud, the stretching wings.

SERMON OF THE HILLS

in Tuscany

We are voices but never the voices of mountains,
We have dignity but never condescend,
The good trees burst in flower and fruit upon us,
And the olive prepares its oil and the vineyard loves us;
They speak of us quietly, mostly in the spring.

There are quarries hacked from our many sides,
Oxen who plough out ledges. But the sun,
Ah the sun nests against us in every season's *siesta*.
All are reticent here, almost silent.
But across our valley a little village speaks

And the old and young live their lives in public air.
We are a distance of sky, a channel of water
Entering the silence of men.
So we teach you calm and diffidence but also
Love which sighs from a midnight street for a few,

Love that surrenders day by day at a Mass,
Love that takes the stranger into its calm.
We lean against the sky and all the stars
Are silver flares struck from our many stones.

THE HEART OF NIGHT

Time is a dancer now in the dead of night,
  Spirits dance minuets,
Angels present pavanes under starlight
  And each unsleeper meets

His counter-part, attendant, one who knows
  The steps by heart. How much
The sleepers miss in ignorant repose
  Of small hours' magic touch.

But they have their own time. It is the dawn.
  Flights are the movements then.
Stars have thinned out and all the dancers gone
  Back to the mood of angels, or of men.

ARRIVAL IN BIBBIENA, TUSCANY

A huddle of shadows and
Small lights down all the slopes. Dark had come down
And we were racing now through the sweet warmth
Of Tuscany with its slit moon
And its imperial crown.

How fitting it is always to arrive
By night in foreign places. They give hints
Of royalty tomorrow, sovereign sun
At its full height, but now it was the moon,
A goddess, a madonna with full hands

Offering simple, therefore holy things.
Her child had gone to sleep as we drew near
Our destination. No need now to speak.
No words were needed, simply being there,
And feeling night's soft arms, was strong and dear.

REMEMBERING BIBBIENA IN TUSCANY

Green hills assemble in this Northern dawn.
The first birds whisper and there is a haze
Suggesting heat. O Tuscan hills draw near,
Counsel my memory. You walk to me
In a strange landscape, English in a summer
Not seen till June. You churches,

Little Romanesque ones, lend me prayer
When I pass here or enter ugly ones.
What coolness haunted me. It haunts me still
As those brisk swallows did in Tuscany.
And then, you friendly people, with loud voices,
Milena and Marino, Sergio,

Enter this English morning. No, you would
Be ill at ease and not at all yourselves.
Stay where you are but draw me back to you
When grapes are trodden and the new wine comes
And you stand there and smile a "Welcome home".

A KIND OF CATALOGUE

Item, a cloud, and how it changes shape,
Now a pink balloon, then a white shift
From a Victorian doll. The forms won't keep
One pattern long. Item, a flow of wind
Carrying dust and paper, gathering up

Rose petals. Item, a command of sun
Subtly presented on a lifted face,
A shaft of light on leaves, darkness undone
And packed away. Item, limbs moved with grace,
Turning the air aside. Item, my own

Observations, now *Lot This, Lot That*
Ready for an unseen auctioneer.
The bidders are half-conscious choices met
To haggle. Signs are made, sometimes I hear
My whisper bidding for *Lot This, Lot That*.

SPARROW

The hallowed, the special flyer, I mean the sparrow,
A flash of feathers and tiny body, a quick
Nerve, a spirit of speed and certainly one
To copy when you are tempted to turn from the sun.
Sparrow of "special providence" teach to us
Your joy, your gladness, your success, for you
Live in accord with that power which moves
You fast and far. Your flights and pauses bring
Delight to us. We are not surprised you were chosen
Specially, for even birds who sing
With a rapture of angels lack your flare and fling.

FIELD-MOUSE

Pause for a moment. Look
At the poised power of the universe which holds
    All things in place. No book
Telling of earth or sky describes those fields
    Which are ready now to break

    Corn, make the harvest start.
Observe the purpose everywhere—that man
    Who is about to set
The combine harvester to its business. It can
    Work quickly, is a threat

    To the field-mouse hearing sound
Come nearer and nearer. He is stiff with fear,
    He has so little ground
To stand on. He will go under the harvester
    And never be found, or mourned.

BLACKBIRD SINGING

Out of that throat arise
  Such notes of poignant sound
That circle round the skies
  And never come to ground.

The bird has gone elsewhere
  But its melody echoes on
Through the transported air
  And it even gilds the sun.

Can any of us be
  So utterly outside our
Personal city
  Or the treading of the hour?

Never. O let it go
  On, this blackbird's song.
It has so much to show
  Our weakness. It is strong

But at least we recognize,
  Innocence, purity,
There is eloquence in the sky's
  Space and sweet energy.

NOT MINE

Take my hands, full moon, take my
Aspirations. Take my hope,
You stars that spread the sky
And I can feel my scope
For joy increasing but it is not "I"

Any longer. I am lost in leaves
Falling and staying. In the harvest I
Gathered the corn with power
Of memory and imaginings. I beg,
I cannot stop it, that the last full hour

Of summer stay with me till spring next year.

OVER AND OVER

Over and over they suffer, the gentle creatures,
The frightened deer, the mice in the corn to be gathered,
Over and over we cry, alone or together.
And we weep for a lot we scarcely understand,
Wondering why we are here and what we mean
And why there are huge stars and volcanic eruptions,
Earthquakes, desperate disasters of many kinds.
What is the answer? Is there

One? There are many. Most of us forget
The times when the going sun was a blaze of gold
And the blue hung behind it and we were the whole of awe,
We forget the moments of love and cast out time
And the children who come to us trusting the answers we
    give
To their difficult and important questions. And there

Are shooting stars and rainbows and broad blue seas.
Surely when we gather the good about us
The dark is cancelled out. Mysteries must
Be our way of life. Without them we might
Stop trying to learn and hoping to succeed
In the work we half-choose and giving the love we need.

RESCUED

These are the many but they must be praised.
They have known dark valleys but have raised
Their eyes to rings of stars. They have climbed up
Hill-sides and cliffs and felt the vertigo
Of height but have gone on, not looked below
But watched the sky and rested at the top.

Do not imagine these have never been
In *cul de sacs* of near-despair and seen
Death as desirable. They have and they
Have turned away from it. It is good luck
Simply to be and these have turned their back
On the dark stranger who stands in the way

Of life, the breath of it, its primal power
Settled in us, with each one given our
Specific strength. That stranger's had his toll
Of many lost. Some were nearly so
But brought back by great mercy. This I know
For I gave up but felt a great power pull

Me back and now I see why and am glad,
Also ashamed. Call that power God,
As I do, call it fortune. I have found
Some use in all those shadows. They have told
Me of the terror that makes dying bold
But now I hear its soft retreating sound.

AN ELEGY BEFORE DEATH

for two old ladies aged 94 and 101

They cannot die and they would like to go
On the quiet ferry, slipping out of this world.
They've led rich lives, each differently so.
Onto this life each keeps a careful hold.
     What can my words do?

I'll give an elegy to see them through
The last few stretches. I shall have to say
"We love you still. We cannot bear that you
Should want to leave us every opening day."
     These words are partly true

But, secretly, I want what these two want
For themselves—a happy drifting off
Into other worlds they trust. We can't
Say that we want what they want now. Our love
     Has to lie. These haunt

Our imaginations. We say we
Need them. We mean it but we realize
We must sound selfish, never let them see
That we can see their own world with their eyes
     But cannot set them free.

CHILDREN AT PLAY

"And I shall be a tree,"
The child said to a playmate. He went on,
"You are the river I am growing near,"
And to a third he said, "You are the boat
Which rows across my clear, fresh water." So
The ring-leader decided and the game
Went on for days, for weeks. Sometimes a word

Was heard by parents who looked baffled. They
Had quite forgotten how imagination
Had worked with them once. Certainly some have
More intense ones but there can be few
Children who lack some small creative power
Which is how an imagination shows
Itself. But it grows dim. That boy who played

At trees and rivers grew up with no gift
For any art but he became adept
At science and computers. Now he has
Children who, in a year or two, will play
The kind of game he knew. Will he forget
Just how it felt or be quite otherwise,
Feel the cold shudder of a large regret?

LANDSCAPES AND FIGURES

Have you seen a landscape where the people
Do not fit? We always tend to think
Of paintings where, perhaps, a loving couple
Gives the foreground a small, careful link
    With the clouds that topple

Over the mountains in the whole landscape.
Painters are clever. They compose the scene.
It's true that real landscapes sometimes keep
People suited to the place but then,
    Too often they will step

Out of the picture, play no part in what
The trees discourse about, the winds supply.
We jostle for our place and few will not
Try to keep the background from the eye.
    We ought to be taught

The selflessness of figures in a Claude.
They take us to the hazy sky beyond.
They are to hills and sky what a prelude
Is to dramatic music. A background
    Teaches a moral you'd

Hardly expect. But surely a concern
With people, with the land they live in are
The way we lose ourselves. From art we learn
To step back and be self-effacing where
    Dawn enters, sunsets burn.

HEYDAY

All was a blossom and a bounty then,
A world of learning pulsing with the young
Keen minds at work, quick eyes to speed to eyes,
Libraries of the great to move among
And all those dazzling, wondering young men.

Enough to turn your head. It never did.
I had my flowering too but it came late.
I was surprised into the magic of
Party or ball, the passionate and sweet
Moment of young men moving into love

And moving me, young too. This one would shine
With love of art and read his poetry,
That one was shy and when he first kissed me
It was a child's touch. Vulnerability
Belonged to all of us. I hid in mine.

Only as it went slowly (an eclipse
Would have been kinder) did I realize
How much admired I was, what careful grace
And disguised awkwardness there were. Such eyes
Followed me far, and then the meeting lips.

LEAVES IN THE WIND

Wind muddles energy
But yet brings us the shape and power of peace.
There are tides in each tree.
These could be waves turned by the wind, and this
Could well be an unpeopled world. Such free

Abandonments there are
But there is regularity also.
Rushing upon my ear
The leaves of ash and chestnut, oak now flow
And bring the summer tokens of the year.

All is a gentle dance.
Dark green of fir and paler shades suggest
The varying Aegean's
Gamut of night-blue, turquoise and the rest.
The wind lifts, alters, and has all the means

To show all hues. So here
It is with green. The air is green, the light
Is mixed with green. The sheer
Strength of winds has now a friendly fight
Until the night when all shades disappear.

AFTERWARDS

After I've climbed the ladders to the dark
Sky and viewed the stars, after I
Have gone down to a sea where the waves work

In their old custom but more quietly
At this time of the year, after this
I shall find a content that's meant to be

A present for another. Who, then, is
This other? I don't know yet, may not know
For months or years till I see happiness

In someone else who tells me they must show
Some peace they've found—a white roll of the sea,
A gull upon a ledge, a sun bent low

Or something else I never dreamt could be
Until I recognize it, a design
I started but now working quietly

A life which could not when it was still mine.

IMAGES OF LOVE

First Love

A fist of red fire, a flower
Opening in the sun. A kind of peace
Taking over at last, and then the quick release.

Grief

Pull down the tokens. Close your eyes,
Hide from the sun. At least the night
Will keep the pain from other people's sight
And you'll have the stars' cold light.

FIRST ADMIRERS

In those early days it was a game.
   I didn't know the rules
This didn't matter. I lived in a dream
Of love. So many love poems and love tales

Turned out to be quite true at this beginning.
   The world shone clear for me.
There was no trickery or any cunning.
Men admired me and I honestly

Do not think I toyed or trifled with
   Their feelings. Very soon
One would wound me. Love can be dark beneath
This sweet long dance, the working of the moon.

THE NEAR PERFECTION

This was all sweet and leaping, reciprocal,
Love took off from ground and we were two
Fitted together in body and mind also.
Compassion crowned the royal state of love,
This glory of the senses when they are
Controlled, the eager longing that the other
One should always share
Or more than share this love which did indeed
Happen at first sight. Two summers through
Love was our city and our state of mind,
It painted and it lit up everyone
But all was broken and I don't know why,
Perhaps I thought perfection could endure.
That kind of love, I think, belongs to spring.
We had two springs, were lucky with such power.

GIVEN AN APPLE

He brought her an apple. She would not eat
And he was hurt until she said,
"I'm keeping it as a charm. It may
Grow small and wrinkled. I don't care.
I'll always think of you today.
Time is defeated for that hour
When you gave me an apple for
A love token, and more."

A PLACE TO WALK IN

It was a time of peace and people went
About in quiet groups and pairs. It was
A formal world. It seemed a starting-place.
In fact it had been wasteland rife with weeds
And broken glass, the debris of a world
Torn by war and pain.

But time and clever minds and subtle fingers
Cleaned that place up, lit huge bonfires there,
Carried off stones and, when the ground was soft,
They planted seeds and shrubs, set evergreen
And deciduous trees there, and there they
Placed statues, follies, fountains, everything

To soothe the eye and cool the feverish brain.
I walked once through this garden with you and,
Although we seldom spoke, I felt a close
Pleasure link us together, yours and mine.
Wordless, we took each other's hand and walked
In from the twilight to the waiting feast.

SONG OF LOVE AND PEACE

Love, be a bird to me,
   Lullaby me, wake
Me to the dawn and the
   Voices of day-break.

Love, I will sing you to
   A sleep dividing us.
I'll wake you to the true
   Dawn, day's impetus.

Love, let us wind round
   Each other silence, peace
Deeper than silence. Sound
   Is far away from us.

Morning we'll enter with
   The birds. When shall we speak?
Not till the first bird's breath
   Sings us wide awake.

LAND OF PLENTY

And there was the land of plenty.
We stood upon the edge, the frontier,
We saw the apple-blossom and the roses,
We saw the wholesome green of every vineyard.
We watched the cypresses, steadfast in winter,
Now giving shade to any who desired it.

A land of plenty—that goes back as far
As "when my ship comes in". We have passwords,
Keepsake language, ciphers, symbols but
Here are rich stems of tulips, here is sap
Denying gravity. We wait a cautious
Moment before we cross this frontier,
As if we trespassed on gifts undeserved.

WHAT WE REMEMBER

What we remember are not curves of sun
Or swing of bells or orchestra or band,
What we remember of that day is one
Pure flight of nameless birds above the land
And all the afternoon

Unwinding slowly, golden thread above
Impartial grass, wild flowers that nod in heat.
We lay in the extreme repose of love
And everywhere we looked there was complete
Fruition and enough

Of everything for everyone. That day,
That thread of gold, our hands linked loosely are
A keepsake for the time when things don't play
Together. There was then a door ajar
To Eden or Cathay.

PEACE

A little peace is luck, a trance,
    A spell, a sacrament.
A dove drops feathers. Children chance
    Upon them. Keep them, paint

Them red or green. The bird's away
    As feathers fall, so peace
Comes sparingly. The dove can't stay
    Long in a single place.

And this is prayer or part of it,
    The white shape in the mind.
The feather touch of God will let
    In light that will not blind

And will not last. The rest is work,
    The world's need of us, each
His talent in the sun and dark
    Then, perhaps, peace's touch.

AN UNNERVING LESSON

Take what you will of me. What most appeals
    Among my qualities
Of good and evil? Learn me, what is false
And self-deceiving. Then remember this,

I can shadow, even echo you.
    We two half-strangers yet
Are drawn together. Say why this is so.
I am lingering and prepared to wait

Night and day. What puzzles you? Are you
    Afraid of me? I will admit
I can scare myself and often do.
Not love, not hate and not indifference set

Us together. In a looking-glass
    I have been staring. Then
I went into a fairground where the glass
Grotesquely can distort us. Out again

I go and first avoid all mirrors but
    I look again and see.
Nothing is there, no face. I should look out.
Shall I then find what I thought once was me?

IMPERFECTION

The causes and the questionings of love
I have moved through again. They do not pause
And I do not grow out of them. I move

Ahead in love and there's no winning tape.
In fact, the race of love will never end.
It seems to play with us. We try to keep

It, hoard it. This is always wrong. Our friends
Sometimes run upon a different track
From ours and no one wholly understands

The shifts, the thrusts, the griefs in us. We lack
Much that seems essential for deep love,
But now and then two will find a trek

Only they know. O may we also move
More often where the sun itself can break
Into huge blossoms, starlight in their wake.

A DARK PASSION

I can remember that obsessive love,
Passion, paradoxically, played
Little part in it. Desire was of
A reasonable strength yet I was frayed
And fretted by a rough,

Bullying power. If there had been a foe
That I could see, no doubt I would have fought
This dark obsession, but it did not show
In any form. The person I was caught
Up by did not know

What he was causing. In a curious way
He was not relevant or, rather, was
A channel through which ran this cruel play
With me, my heart. I knew there was no grace
And no repose. Today,

I still know little more of that odd passion
Except that later feelings I'm drawn by
Are clear to me. I do not want possession.
Did I have to know that dark so I
Might love like all creation

Growing now daily? Like one out of prison,
I find sun is my garment, thought the sky.

RECOVERING FROM A DEATH

We are back with our disorders again.
Last year's death has moved into the dark,
For with a real death the shadows drain
Away. All is exact and pure and stark.
     Fear of death has been

Among us since the final mourning seeped
Away. So fear, it seems, is healthy. We
Creep, stride, manoeuvre, once again are kept
Afraid. I think we miss the dignity
     Of mourning. We were stripped

Of all pretence. Love showed its proper size,
Small circumstances drifted quietly off.
Not to mourn can be a loss. We prize
A perfect grief, an almost selfless love
     And wide, defenceless eyes.

WORDS ABOUT GRIEF

Grief can return without a warning. It's
    Seldom cemeteries
Or news of other deaths that my grief fits
But places of great beauty where I was,

However briefly, happy with the one
    I loved who died. I know
Many feel happier when again they've gone
To such a place with grief. One thing I do

Know is that after years grief brings a pang
    As terrible almost
As that first rending. Death, where love's been strong,
Can always make you feel entirely lost

Or so it does with me. Time does not heal,
    It makes a half-stitched scar
That can be broken and again you feel
Grief as total as in its first hour.

FOR A GENTLE FRIEND

I have come to where the deep words are
Spoken with care. There is no more to hide.
I toss away the cold stance of my fear

And move O far, far out to be beside
One who owns all language in extremes
Of death. We watch the coming-in now tide.

We have lived through the nightmares death presumes
To wound us with. We faced the darkest place.
Death the familiar enters all our rooms.

We wear its colour. Its mask's on our face.
But not for long. It's good to let tears run.
This is the quick, the nerve, also the grace

Of death. It brings our life into the sun
And we are grateful. Grief is gracious when
It takes the character of this kind one,

This gentle person. We re-live his life
And marvel at the quiet good he's done.

A HAND LIFTING

A hand lifting the leaves and the leaves turning
In the sun. The hand is a child's. It goes
On exploring. It has not yet learnt
All it cannot know and may not do.
Our hands were like that once. I thought that you

Knew me as we can learn a continent
By touching cities on a turning globe.
We did not make demands much then and so
Were not disappointed. Now you rub

The tears from your red eyes. Like you I can
See that love must be an elegy.
However hard we try or well we plan
We stand apart before death has its way.

That is why death is terrible. It breaks
The little links we make. Were they more strong
Grief would be great but would not last so long
Since what's joined totally and wholly breaks

Makes a clean severance, an open wound.
It can be healed and comforted also.
But what has not been wholly joined is found
Not wholly parted. Our lot makes this so.

IS IT DUAL-NATURED?

Is it dual-natured to be so alive
Sometimes that your flesh seems far too small
To contain the power of the sun, or how stars thrive,

But then to be diminished, become a small
Dark of yourself, yourself your hiding-place
Where you converse with shadows which are tall

Or listen to low echoes with no grace
Of lyric joy or calm? I do not feel
Divided deep. Sometimes, the sense of the place

Where I am most light and eager can make me thrill
To the planet's course. I am pulled or do
I draw myself up, into the sun's overspill?

One or other. It only matters I know
What levitation would be and am grateful to learn
What's instinctive to birds is what makes the wind blow.

I will risk all extremes. I will flounder, will stumble, will
      burn.

PAINTER FROM LIFE

He stands close to a rock. Where light falls as
The painter needs it, he
Has set his model. Now and then he asks
The youth to move, and he will keep his pose
Though sea-sounds mock his stance, while gulls go free

Over this little group. There's not a voice,
Two men exchanging thoughts and moods. They are
Almost one person for a second, then
The painter asks for movement. Here is true
Creation shared. The silent art of paint

Is now surrounded by the tempting sea,
The shafts of sun, the hot sand and the gulls.
Nature and art show here,
Briefly, all things as they were meant to be.

WORDS FOR MUSIC

A voice on a drift of wind,
An echo left behind,
A star in one pane of glass,
    An act of grace,

The child's farewell to day,
The old with wisdom we
Recognize, the rose
    Unplucked—for verse

These can be metaphors
Or, perhaps, words of praise,
The world is moving fast,
    Poets are hard-pressed,

But at the day's end there is
A silence to fit peace,
Moments when words ring true
    And love also.

A KIND OF MAGIC

The trees walk, they peer through the summer haze,
    The roses unfold their skin,
Chestnut candles glimmer. On such good days
Summer's not only around us but within

Our thoughts and it plays there. I have walked through
    A wood and gathered its light,
The last gleam of the sun before it must go
Into the territory of the night.

Magic thought of is a true event.
    It happens in the mind.
It is imagination never spent,
It is the warmth that lonely people find.

Everything we think takes on unseen
    Happiness or grief.
Not only mystics have interior lives.
Most have a little in a usual life,

But when it comes to God, how magic thrives.

THE ONE DRAWBACK

It stays, it stays. I have incalculable
Hours of supreme sun, light which always can
Draw me on, running with light, draw me on
In somebody else's plan
But the movement is my own.

I should expect dark to be given when
I have such lights, some are tall as the sun,
Others are hearths which friends will sit around.
When these lights have gone
I am drawn underground.

I wander there but break sometimes into
A run. I only tire myself, I wait,
Imagining summers of another world.
To move in dark is a fate
But I know also the gold

Dawns of the world outside me, and within
Dawns in which words break into fresh song,
My mind is raided by a dazzling light,
Sun is where I belong
But I'm an expert on night.

I CAME ONCE

I came once into a field of love.
I knew it was because I felt my heart
Beating faster. Softly, I would move

And noticed nimbuses of light were part
Of all I looked at. There were curious shapes
I'd never seen before. These shapes would start

Up anywhere. Sometimes clouds from scraps
Of broken cloudlets came together in
A stretch of satin near the sun. Great leaps

Into the sky, a flash of birds, would win
Over the wind, it seemed. All this I know
Because a love in me that leapt within

My heart found an exchange, another who
Wordlessly smiled, silently took my hand.
This is a magic we have no power to

Call up. We're happy not to understand.

AS THE ROOKS ARE

Alone as the rooks are
In their high, shaking homes in the sky at the mercy of
    winds,
Alone as the lurking trout or the owl which hoots
Comfortingly. I have a well-crammed mind
And I have deep-down healthy and tough roots

But in this house where I live
In one big room, there is much solitude,
Solitude which can turn to loneliness if
I let it infect me with its darkening mood.
Away from here I have an abundant life,
Friends, love, acclaim and these are good.

And I have imagination
Which can travel me over mountains and rough seas;
I also have the gift of discrimination.
High in a house which looks over many trees
I collect sunsets and stars which are now a passion.
And I wave my hand to thousands of lives like this,
But will open my window in winter for conversation.

SOURCES OF LIGHT

SOURCES OF LIGHT (I)

a sonnet

Sources of light and arbiters of men,
From torch to star, from moon to candle-flame,
In the bad hour of unexpected pain,
In the good hour of Christ's holy name,

These are the lights that turn into the Word,
The anxious query and assenting voice,
This is the universe's cradled Lord,
The litany from depths which still rejoice.

So light is language, so the stars give tongue,
So noon is voices babbling in the heat,
Or in the Polar snows all praise is sung.

We are delivered as we sit to eat
Our daily bread. Our God's for ever young
And he has all the planets at his feet.

MANY RELIGIONS

Spring is inexhaustible, I swear
    In early March it's on
Us already. Morning sky is clear.
There is no winter garment on the sun.

Can we catch up? We move with quickened steps,
    We breathe an air that's new.
Surely now no hibernator sleeps.
Are migrants back, small arrows on the blue

Stretch of sky? Not yet, but any hour
    They'll come in strict formation.
Meanwhile we stretch our limbs and feel new power,
We too take part in this regeneration.

Eyes become brighter as the evenings come
    Later each night. We stare
At the sky opening. It waits for some
Arrival. Christ and Proserpine are near,

There's no blasphemy in this. All old
    Beliefs are sewn into
One great tapestry. Tales new and old
Are woven there. Like night dreams coming true.

LET US

Let our hands be raised and held
In attentive silence. Let
Our minds be wholly stilled
And we be whole. O let
Us feel the fibres of
The universe, the shape
Of so much life, and love.

How smoothly the world rounds
The sun through day, through night.
Even the stars make sounds
For there's eloquence in Light.
We kneel, we stand, we embrace,
We feel the pulse of the world
And Christ is on our breath
As we move on to death.

PRAYER

A flame, another element, a law
Made by experimental joy and care,
A world of golden roses, end of war,
A place of many kinds is personal prayer.
        Each one at the core

Is different as we are to the bone.
Much we have in common, it is true,
But they are obvious things. We have alone
Our kind of prayer, our own approaches to
        God who comes in his own

Way to us that suits our natures and
Capacity. To some he is a king
Dispensing property. He is a hand
That begs to others. I have heard him sing
As a child does, and I understand
        He comes to me to bring

Me out of turning-inward and to play
Which is important if it is well done.
This child walks close beside me on a day
Of curious magic. I had never known
        This was a way to pray.

FIRST SUNDAY IN LENT AT DOWNSIDE

Love back in Bread. Rome back, a certain church,
A hill long loved there. Christ, it's Lent, I know,
But you have come to me and not to teach
But tell me of the dread despair you know.
You say, "I am in reach,

I know your wilderness, I know the threat
Of tempting, and the pleasant way it feels
To hear the devil's whisper easy, sweet,
Offering you rich kingdoms, also false
Luxury. I meet

You in the hot and tempting hour but I
Have another world, another way
To live. I've been your child. You neighboured me.
Have you forgotten all that Christmas day
You held me on your knee?"

I am amazed. The voices rise, the light
Pours through the windows. Christ, your Lenten gift
Raises my heart. I have a sudden sight
Of Calvary. O let me, please, be left
Present at the sight

Of your triumphant dereliction. Lord,
This Lent's first Sunday is a joyful time.
I know the whole of Easter. Your good word,
Saviour, again forgives all mankind's crime.
Child, let my prayer be heard.

A MEMORY AND A FACT IN EARLY LENT

All the bells rang again. In Rome they rang
In a Sunday serenade of God, a song
In every church was being sung at Mass
And Christ came now concealed in Bread but in
Triumph totally. He cancelled sin
As fast as sorrow, and it seemed he was

In every Mass living his whole life through
Again, was born, grew up in me and you
And everyone who sang and meant his Creed.
This was in Rome now twenty years ago
But this morning I met him again. He took me to
His joy and grief. I felt my spirit grow

And burst in flame, a meteor that would
Not flash out quickly. In the Holy Bread
The world's pulse beat, creation was contained
And I was back within my proper place,
Happy to tears, glad to be sorry when grace
Filled me. To Christ's life I had returned

So courteously. His hands were held out to
Mine, his thought spoke in me and I knew
His presence as momentous yet as part
Of every coming day. O God, your heart
Broke mine today and I'm glad of the hurt
For I'm restored, am trusted and made new.

THE ENDLESS CRUCIFIXION

I cannot bear the swearing and the flies,
The blood, the mutilation and the sweat,
For you, my Lord and God. My master dies,
His body torn, his bleeding hands and feet.
His cries are a child's cries

And so we move now from Jerusalem
And go back through his ministry, back far
To his humble birth in Bethlehem.
The Wise Men would be too old to be here
But they knew Christ. In him

They saw more than a special man or king.
They knelt and wise men only kneel to God.
Christ, you suffer still for each bad thing
Done by any. Please forgive me, good
Lord. The darkening

Sky is turning into storm. Strange lights,
Gaudy, grim and yellow clouds smoke. Now
Christ's side is pierced. He dies. O to what heights
Is he delivered? His hands on this Tree's boughs,
His friends release him. Rites

Of burial are performed. This all went on
Long ago but it's repeated when
We try to mend ourselves and change this one
Violent, unhappy world. It is in pain.
Jesus, thy will be done.

MANY EASTERS

Do any escape the dark garden and
The high hill under the hazy afternoon sun?
Do any remain only in coolness and stand
In the sun- or moon-light? Surely, surely, none.
For all must comprehend

The big as the small sadness. Most don't know
Whence it comes or why it does or if
It will go and never return. Even though
The time is short, unhappiness very brief
A lesson is learnt. We go

By different routes and at different times and yet
Reach the tall hill and the strange trees, with one
Specially tall. A figure has been put
To hang there still and this has all been done
By all of us. There's no doubt

About the responsibility. A God
Long ago, out of our time's calculation,
Gave us freedom and we made the bad
Choice. In his huge creating imagination
He decided he would

Send his son, also God, to die
To save us for himself. The love we know
Is a faint shadow of this but to Calvary
We must all come some day, somehow, and must show
Our sorrow. Again we,

Like many before, bury this dead God,
Plant him in earth, bind him round until
The spring comes and one flower white and red
Flourishes. It has a meaning to tell.
It is the Word, Our Lord.

SIMPLICITIES

Not only present in the life of hills
And trees and meadows and the stirring sea
And in men's characters and in each sense
And element, and instinct of the beasts,
Not only here, Lord, are you present, though,
Should you withdraw your power all would fall
And disappear and nothingness be here.

But Lord, to make things simple, easy for our so
Easily frightened hearts you came to us
In Bread, the simplest form, our daily Bread.
Always simplicity attended your
Activities. O yes, we know that you
Gave a sense of glory which you can
And do at all times satisfy—the fire,
The flame of God's great Trinity, the sung

Mass, the recited Hours, the natural world's
Views and glories. Yes, we find you there
But in our shyer moments we prefer
To see you in a cradle sleeping fast
And find you in the Bread no one could fear.

THE VOICES OF PLAIN CHANT

There are the deep notes which come from dark places,
They rise slowly, they draw black spirits up
Until they climb the ladder of the chants.
Then there are high notes,

They have been surely struck by star on star
Like flint on flint on earth,
These voices need no ladders, we are with
Their heights at once, for spring has coincided
With Lent's first Sunday. Easter will be late.

Then there are voices bidding, wooing, pleading.
What heart's so cold it can ignore this sound?
What spirit is so evil it can stay
Shadowing all round it? Few, O, few,
For now come lower voices, voices which
Whisper of penitence. One thought of sorrow
And we are carried up by choirs of such
Ecstatic heights, we find we love our lost
Innocence which is closing in again.

I BEG FOR LIGHT

I beg, I ask for light,
 Candle, lantern, the shine
Of children's eyes at night,
 Light is always a sign

Of energy, of man's
 Ride through the universe
Under the sun and moon's
 Rise and falling course.

Love is light also,
 Light that candles us
Through the labyrinth where we go
 Upon our final course.

SOURCES OF LIGHT (II)

a sonnet

Gold, all shimmerings, and all excess
Of light, entrances most of us. We cry
At the world's dazzle when we're born but this
Only reveals how sensitive we lie

Under our first shafts of the sun. We grow
Into the well-worn gold, the reach of shine.
Companionable shadows help to show
Their opposites. For most light is a sign

Of peace and benediction. Think how sky
Threatened the world's dark when a frightened few
Heard their hanging master's last great cry

And watched his end and what seemed our end too.
But Christ rose with the sun on Easter Day.
He was the true word and true light also.

OVER AGAIN

a litany

To the child who lay under a steadfast star
Let there be warmth and sleep,
To the girl who bore a child who would change the world,
Let us always keep
A vigil with and for her. She can drive
Dark thoughts off. With melancholy ones
She smiles and her light makes the shadows dance.
Now I hear men drive

Nails into a pale man's hands and feet,
They've put a crown of thorns insultingly
Upon his head. The sky goes dark. Again
Christ cries across the sky and shakes the world
For God by God seems for a moment doubted.
And mankind holds its breath.

No one is forsaken, all is well
And saved and peaceful. Make the most of still
Times not times like this. Now, through the air
A young girl's voice is singing, but from where
We cannot judge and do not need to tell.